The Invitation

Joyce Åkesson

Pallas Athena

Lund

2009

The Invitation

All Rights Reserved

Copyright © 2009 by Joyce Åkesson

2009 Pallas Athena Distribution, Skarpskyttevägen 10 A, 226 42 Lund, Sweden.

Book design by Joyce Åkesson

This book may not be reproduced, stored in a retrieval system or transmitted in any form or by any means, electronic, mechanical, photocopying, recording, scanning or otherwise without the prior permission of the Publisher except in the case of brief quotations embodied in critical articles and reviews.

ISBN: 978-91-977641-4-8

PRINTED IN THE UNITED STATES OF AMERICA

ALSO BY JOYCE ÅKESSON

Love's Thrilling Dimensions, Pallas Athena Distribution, February 2009.

Majnūn Leyla: Poems about Passion, Pallas Athena Distribution, December 2009.

The Complexity of the Irregular Verbal and Nominal Forms & the Phonological Changes in Arabic, Pallas Athena Distribution, April 2009.

Arabic Morphology and Phonology: Based on the Marāḥ al-Arwāḥ by Aḥmad b. ᶜAlī b. Masᶜūd, Studies in Semitic Languages and Linguistics, Brill Academic Publishers, July 2001.

Aḥmad B. ᶜAlī B. Masᶜūd on Arabic Morphology, Marāḥ al-Arwāḥ: Part 1: The Strong Verb, Studia Orientalia Lundensia, Vol. 4, Brill Academic Publishers, October 1990.

CONTENTS

Perhaps	1
Interventions	3
Transformations	5
The Invitation	8
Soul and Body	10
Movement	12
The Art of Living	14
Longing	15
Traveler	16
A Refuge	18
Complexities	20
Intrusions	22

Eyes	24
Man's Dignity	26
Love's Essence	29
Attunement	31
Awareness	32
Expectations	34
Sublimation	36
Lights	38
Reflections	39
Interactions	41
Meeting	42
The Substitute	43
Mutual Feelings	46
In Spinoza's World	47
No Butterfly Effect	49
The Adolescent Orphan	51
The Secret Mirror	54
The Adventurer	56

Plans	58
A Possible Encounter	59
Fire	61
Taking The World As It Comes	64
In Your World	65
The Power Of Imagination	67
The Dream	70
Stagnation	74
Waiting for Godot	75
Conflicts	79
Absurdism And Realism	83
Somewhere In This World	85
Memories	87
Some Go And Come	90
Questions About Love	91
Searching For A Poem	94
Solace	98
The Magical Days	100

Past And Current Potential Lives	102
Inanimate Things	107
Drive	109
Reflections	112
Possibilities	116

The Invitation

PERHAPS

Perhaps that this is a changing
and ever-lasting world,
that its houses get repeatedly demolished
and its towns deserted,

that it is a chaos of men and women,
dancing to the symphonies
of a capricious blue moon,

that its images get blurred and disappear
before that a pale sun
clicks on the remote control
and drinks itself to oblivion
to its bewildering beauty.

Perhaps that love goes well with the rain
and music with broken glass,

that the flowers have their numerous souls
and the eyes their hidden pasts,
and that the night smells
of wet grass and ideal warmth.

Perhaps that I am an idealistic prisoner of a perfect life,
that the roads multiply in the fog
and the days have their enchanting lights,

>that the birds sing
>and the children play,
>and a lover never fails
>to appear in the dark.

INTERVENTIONS

Cosmic disturbances,
electromagnetic waves moving in a void.

A blending of sparks, colors and sounds,
a contact between the speed of light,
the law of gravity,
the end and the beginning.

Diverse sparks and ashes,
new codes and rites,
different pleasures and warnings,

and the awkward feeling
of a misunderstood understanding,
a misinterpreted interpretation,
a meaning lost in translation,

an engulfing memory,
a word-blind emotion.

Feelings and thoughts tumbling
across a choppy and linear language
over the threshold of the Unknown,

> *similar to adventurous separate entities,*
> *touching and abandoning each other*
> *on familiar and foreign territories.*

TRANSFORMATIONS

Synchronic dreams,
telepathic questions and visions,

an imaginary paradise
before our expecting sights.

Water evaporating,
worries dissipated,
emotions generated.

The world wanders
with wide-opened eyelids
through different tunnels and lights.

6

The sun's rays and the winds,
here and there over the fields,
amid beings
and faceless trees.

Time is a wave,
moving from the sea to the shore,
backwards and forwards.

The light becomes a shadow
that becomes a light
and then another shadow,
and then a light.

The day and night
reconcile at midnight.

The sun takes a break in a sunset
at the time when the horizon hides it in its womb
before giving birth to it at dawn.

An echo resonates with another echo
in another dimension.

From one world to another,
the force of attraction is eternity.

THE INVITATION

I sense cheerful moods
and compatible signals,
and this meeting matters very much to me.

So I thank you for the invitation
and for all the generous information
that you are sharing about yourself
and the world you are living in.

My imagination is at work.
You are on the alert.

I shall take all the initiatives to please you.
You can weave the continuity.

I shall interpret the different signs
that you have left all over the place for me.

From one word to another,
there is a divine constellation,
a magical rainbow,
an overflowing light.

Their charm resides in their fiery rhymes
and the particular intonations
that conjunct so well
with my most secretive dreams.

SOUL AND BODY

Our soul is of the nature of air,
weightless, formless,
undefined in the void,
rootless, nameless,
untouched by the invisible hands of time,
undistinguishable from other souls.

Our body is of the nature of earth,
concrete, shaped,
distinct, with contours,
center and gravity,
separated from other bodies,
participating in groups,
contributing to situations,
moving in a linear time,
living in a reality full of doors,

windows, mirrors, stars and beings,

affected by the rigorous light,

subjected to the laws of time,

experiencing success and failures,

changing and ageing before turning to dust.

MOVEMENT

The enormous eye of time
unveils the appearances,

transforms the presence
into the absence of being,

renders the undecipherable clear,
dissolves the fixed center,

throws a place into a black hole,
creates another time in space,

prolongs the dense silence inward,
drills another incandescent center,

builds a new dimension,
destroys an old galaxy.

Illusions of light and air glisten
in an architecture of waves,

metamorphosis of movements,
journeys between different worlds.

Weightless substances,
air compressed,
faithful shadows,
sun reflections in the halls of mirrors,
faces dissolved in the mist.

> *With half-opened eyelids*
> *our minds travel toward each other*
> *through a space with high-tension wires.*

THE ART OF LIVING

There is a talent in finding
the right information at the right time,
a happiness in pleasing someone else.

Love is the best teacher in this journey.
It is simple:
you take the initiative
and throw the dice.

The knight on the chessboard
remains powerful in closed positions.
You do not have to be afraid of being seasick:
> *the queen behind the keyhole*
> *holds a crown in her hand.*

> *The light flows like the colorless sea.*

LONGING

There are many images scrolling
behind and before you,
a whole life passing,
so much to be learned.

You long for the years spent at the dormitory,
the bright sun and the promising freshness,
the academic positions and occupations,
the weaving of the philosophical truths,
the moon and the bluish landscapes,
the pavilion of the sudden opportunities,
the stranger passing by who became your friend,
the dazzling dawn that keeps on reinventing itself,
the treasure that divided itself in two,
the stars that keep on disappearing and appearing,
the world that keeps on caring for you.

TRAVELER

I lost my sense of time.
I lost sight of the railroad tracks
which lead to my childhood's home.

Have I entered another country,
another era, another world?

It is not the same sky,
the same sun,
the same rain,
the same dew,
the same light,
the same earth.

Have all the stations and trains
fallen into my mind's black hole
or into another parallel dimension
to which I have no access?

All these loved ones,
lonesome passengers
on other trains,
going off in all directions
to unknown destinations
like my own.

Formless figures
without faces or contours,
unrecognizable,
zooming past me,
shrinking into dots,
before vanishing
into other zones.

A REFUGE

There must be a central place
in the well-established scheme of things
that is unreachable for hatred and rage.

A salutary shelter,
an island,
the eye of a storm,
a clarity over an abyss,
a stillness in the procession of time.

A harmonious station.
A secret garden.

An ageless zone
      that drives off cosmic disturbances,
      closes its doors to invaders and conspirators,
      erases evil and pain,

      in which there is no frontier,
      no date, no price,
      no thicket from one spot to another.

It will be like returning to another time,
- perplexing and yet so familiar -.

Our thoughts will be lighter than air,
- and we will feel alive -.

COMPLEXITIES

There are too many days and nights,
too many lights and shadows,
too many entrances and exits,

too many colors shifting and interchanging,
too many lives played on stages,
too many characters avoiding boredom,
    taking risks,
    finding love in abandoned rooms,
    losing themselves in familiar places,
    changed by transformational dawns.

There are too many possibilities and experiences,
too many mouths opening and closing,
too many eyes telling their stories;

Scheherazade's thousand and one nights,
Shahryar's insatiable expectations;

the Queen of Hearts in her house of air,
the King of Spade in his terrace beneath the sun.

INTRUSIONS

There are too many rivers within the same sea,
too many characters within the same scene,
too many images within the same hour,
too man levels within the same dimension,
too many signs within the same path,
too many moments within the same present,
too many actions within the same direction,
too many truths within the same desire,
too many elements within the same constellation,
too many worlds within the same space,
too many islands within the same loneliness,
too many pains within the same darkness,
too many complexities within the same clearness,
too many clarities within the same abyss,
too many thoughts within the same memory,
too many dreams within the same vision,

too many destinations within the same story,

too many presences within the same experience.

EYES

Eyes,

a stranger's,

a friend's,

a lover's,

a door wide open,

a journey from nowhere to everywhere,

an expanding space,

an iridescent darkness,

a light at the end of the tunnel,

a breaking dawn,

a new beginning,

a bond,

an axis,

a lifeline,

an umbilical cord,

a shelter protected from the elements,
a smile clinging to a face.

MAN'S DIGNITY

I once knew a professor,

a supervisor,

a mentor.

a guru.

He said to me: "Life is a riddle.

Happiness is relative.

Finding harmony is a matter of attitude.

Practicing philosophy is a way of interpreting

different truths and attitudes.

Ideals are human fabrications.

The world follows our expectations,

whether good or bad.

An openness of mind is healing.

We must focus on our individual reasoning;

if necessary, cultivate our subterranean thoughts,

work through our dilemmas,

adopt new attitudes,

celebrate our dreams,

keep our sense of self".

He then talked lyrically

about man's upward movement

towards the infinite.

He said: "Nothing in the world matters more

than man's need to elevate himself.

His dignity reflects the adequacy of his knowledge,

the insights he has gained,

the epiphanies he has experienced.

His state is beyond the boundaries of the material.

He deals with abstract concepts,

and sees with his mind's eye

what many others have failed to see.

He creates different works of art,

which express his soul and mind,

and he inspires others with his achievements."

"What about love?" I asked.

"Nothing is possible without love," he answered.

"Love is the master and the path."

LOVE'S ESSENCE

Love's essence
expresses itself in the unity,
in a thirst that cannot be quenched,
in a heat that increases with the fire sparks,
in swelling waves,
in an oasis of calm.

A free soul,
for ever bound
through the flesh and flame.

The source,
the streams,
the passion flowing,
intensified by the full moon.

Elevation of the being.
Sublimation of the concrete.
Life's movement.
Signs exceeding a limit.

Intentions to forget,
to destabilize,
to warm the spirit,
to breathe,
to be reborn
through someone else
- with eyes closed -.

ATTUNEMENT

The space is mute.
We can read each other between the lines.

The passions have been given names,
and in order to preserve them,
we have kept them
hidden in numbered files.

The expanded horizon has dressed itself up in pride.

We can praise each other
and our achievements,
marvel about the sun, the moon,
the planets and the earth,
as the seconds slip by,
slowly, between our fingers.

AWARENESS

There are crucial moments in life
that stretch out like wavelengths
with high frequencies.

Bulbs, a myriad of meteors and stars,
radiate in their magnetic circuits
with heat and light.

Atoms advance through them,
mirrors and transparencies,
different systems of existence,
nature's presence,
the soul's awareness,
colors flowing
through parallel geometries
with uncontrolled movements.

Voices talk clearly
in many languages,
on many different channels
about truths and mysteries;

about the past that is gone
and the future that will come;

about the scattering of unpredictable moments
with their dreams and polarities;

about the rotating world
that protects us from going astray;

about the music that is persistent
and our feelings that are consistent.

EXPECTATIONS

A void that can be filled

conquers a beyond that becomes pervaded.

A night with satin black gloves

caresses the cheeks of the dream.

The moon's seduced gaze

follows life dancing in ballet shoes.

A mind that is open to the infinite

transforms the shadows into trees.

I have put space and time

behind the mask of the concrete.

I have waited for the universe

to be born in my hands.

It has shown me its aura,

its endless and dead spaces.

I have seen its lights,

its distances,

its filled hands,

and all the bridges in between.

SUBLIMATION

There was nothing.

I was alone with my soul.

Now there is everything;

beauty and goodness,

happiness and wisdom.

Everything is clear.

Everything is easy.

Every caress is meaningful.

You surround me.

You are immense.

We are both lost

in the geography of the moment,

We find each other

in the history of our memories.

I live in a wonderful world.

The door is open.

It is morning again.

The light flirts with the world.

I have touched the stars.

LIGHTS

A cloud travels on outside my bedroom's window.

The sunlight dwells for a few hours in my world.

The stained glass gives off a smoldering glow.

The evening darkens.

The dim light of the corridor shows through the keyhole.

The bulb in my lamp springs into life.

The smoke curls up around the room.

You pinch out the cigarette's flame

between your forefinger and your thumb.

The spark of love shines in your eyes.

REFLECTIONS

The wind sings through the pine needles.
The fire is hidden under the earth.

Moving pictures are superimposed,
one over the other,
on life's dim windows.

A corridor of mirrors
moves forward in time.

Different lights, colors and shades
touch the forms, withdraw
and plunge into them repeatedly.

Intangible, transparent,
and yet visible,
the images live a life of their own.

At times broken,
unrecognizable, distorted,
obliterated by an impalpable clarity,
at times resuscitated and intertwined.

A collection of fragments,
carved, put together feature by feature,
perfect copies in their own fragility,
losing themselves in their own reality.

INTERACTIONS

The future draws itself in the mirror.

The silence picks up some unsaid words.

The perfume longs for the invisible flower.

A shadow is born on the pavement.

The light remembers the one who waits for it.

Laughter makes love resonate.

Something is changed:

the gaze precedes the step on the road;

the path is different;

the horizon is vaster;

the mountains are higher.

MEETING

A stranger sits lost on my stairs.

The cosmos is reflected in his eyes.

His mysteries have become attractive to me.

The vision of the absolute is seductive.

The inaccessible is found at the crossroads.

The air is suddenly filled with passion and noise.

Much has now changed under my skies.

The space has become transformative.

The reality unites with my dreams.

THE SUBSTITUTE

We should keep our distances,
but can we keep our principles?

We should not disturb the horizontal horizons:
the seasons' moods are unpredictable.

The measure of the silence is unknown.
The playful days flee like fugitive clouds.

Some memories are easily forgotten.
Some legends are still alive.

A few equations remain ambiguous.
A few rivers have dried up when I was not looking.

Do you know the rules of the game?

Some adventures have become tragic during this season.
I do not know in which direction the wind blows.
There are too many issues that need to be elucidated.

Thoughts and images intertwine
over the threshold of the Unknown.

It was cold, but a few matches warmed me up.
Do you know who lit the fire?

Someone managed to catch my shadow.
I have now a substitute who is walking beside me.

He watches over me and keeps me company.
He sleeps in my bed,
wakes up in my chair,
eats what I eat
and reads what I read.

His life has pages with a preface,

numerous chapters

and footnotes that refer to all my unrevealed secrets.

I do not know anymore how our lives

have become so interconnected.

I am thrilled since it's a beautiful day.

We are going to visit a few temples.

He wants to show me all the stairs, entrances and exits,

and all the rooms with doors, windows and mirrors.

You can join us if you want to.

Do you know what destiny awaits us?

MUTUAL FEELINGS

There is no reason to be weary:
love glows like a candlelight in the dark.

We have the same mutual inclinations,
the same tendencies and potentialities,
the same similar infatuation in a familiar scent,
the same memories returning from distant nights.

The sun is empathic during the days.
Its light pours down generously on the roads.

We have the same great expectations
oriented toward the future.

We live a usual confused life
in two parallel worlds at the same time.

IN SPINOZA'S WORLD

Spinoza states
that the art of controlling one's passions
leads to virtue and happiness.

And I cannot help but wonder
how the world would look like
if we did not feel any deep passion.

We would probably not have Dante's *Inferno*,
Baudelaire's *Artificial Paradise*,
Lautrec's *La Goulue*,
Shakespeare's *Othello*,
the Taj Mahal
or the Pyramids.

Many works of art
and architecture
would not see the day.

The best part would be
that we would not have any war,
- and this in itself is a consolation -.

Moderation would be adapted.
A state of blessedness would be the aim;
a coldness and indifference too.

NO BUTTERFLY EFFECT

A guardian will stand before the door.
No one will escape from these thoughts.
The room will remain locked.

No one will trespass here.
No one will find the prisoner.
No one will seduce the fugitive.

There will be no fire
no smoke,
no storm,
no rain,
no dawn,
no sublimation,
no deception,
no hallelujah,

no fall from grace,
no story,
no future,
no history,
no butterfly effect.

The walls will not talk.
The shadows will not sigh.
The longing hours will just pass.

Everything will remain unchanged.
Everything will stay in its own place,
in a perfect state,
in an undisturbed order.

No love will be awakened.

The name and the word
will remain protected.

THE ADOLESCENT ORPHAN

The adolescent orphan in the social worker's office
talked incessantly about the middle-aged woman
who invited him to live in her luxurious house.

She fed him, bought him expensive clothes
and took him to fancy restaurants.

She did everything to please him:
she cried when he was sad,
laughed when he was glad
and reassured him when he was mad.

She even had his name tattooed on her arm.
All this she did because she loved him.

He was lyrical when he talked about her.
He didn't care about what the social worker thought,
whether he approved of this relation or disapproved.

He felt that he was a man
and that life was treating him well.
As far as he was concerned, the woman was a mother,
a sister, a beloved and a best friend.

At night, he lied beside her in the double bed
and she embraced him before they slept.

He felt lonely. He needed her.
He needed tenderness.

"You need tenderness?" the social worker asked.
The adolescent's eyes blazed when he answered yes.
Yes, yes. He needed tenderness.

Who doesn't need tenderness? The social worker thought.

He envied the boy. He despised him too.

No woman have

 ever loved him this way,

no woman had his name tattooed on her arm.

"All this is wrong," he heard himself say.

"Don't you see what is happening to you?

You cannot stay with this woman.

She's older than you and you're too immature.

We will move you to another place.

You can be sure about that.

This foolishness cannot continue.

What will your poor mother say if she knew?"

THE SECRET MIRROR

I love by excluding.

Is that fair?

Yet my heart is filled with love,

but is this enough?

Seven rays,

seven lights,

seven paths,

seven reasons.

I close my eyes and inhale.

When I open them and exhale

the world is forever changed.

A lover calls me

whom I can only hear.

His voice whispers in my ear:

"You must look into the secret mirror

if you want to see me."

THE ADVENTURER

I have a heart that beats.
You can inhale my breath.

I do not want half the fruit,
I want it all;

the days with the high peaks,
the whirlwinds,
the dizziness,
the sunsets,
the dawns,
the sun's gold,
the moon's silver,
the beaches which are awake,
the mountains in the storm,
the endless fields,

the tolling bells,

the deserted streets,

the dark forests,

the arrivals and the departures,

the smiles and the sighs,

the presence and the absence,

the longing and the reunion,

I want them all.

PLANS

I do not intend to prove anything.
I am still seeking.
I am still longing for the extreme,
for the unspeakable.

I am planning to visit the pyramids,
different amphitheatres, jungles,
mausoleums, museums, castles, mosques, churches,
temples, mountains and valleys.

I am longing to study nature in all its colors:
its energy will keep me warm.

A POSSIBLE ENCOUNTER

Two points
moving toward each other.

Fluid emotions.
Fiery thoughts.

Two transported souls.
Unspoken promises.
A possible encounter.

The universe holds its breath.
Everything moves forward.

Pregnant hours.

Separating sea.

A challenge.

Dreams surfacing.

A world filled with possibilities.

A journey on the invisible path between the stars.

A road taken from the lines of my hand or yours.

An encounter in the fog.

A face that I recognize,
    a face that I have seen before.

        The mist lifted at the right moment.

FIRE

Happiness has wings
and so does love.

A fire flares up
from the center of your world
behind open eyelids,
announcing dreams
flowing like life.

A pillar of light,
a promising light,
different from all the other lights,
strong like a firework erupting into the skies.

An intense heat,

forcing the ice to melt;

outside,

on the flat roads,

on destiny's undiscovered paths,

on the proud mounts,

under the vast horizons,

on the deserted ruins,

on the solid-built houses,

on the ageing buildings,

between the leaves of the trees,

on the waves of the sea,

on the towers,

on the flowers;

inside,

within the frozen moments

hidden in our hands,

preserved in our thoughts;

    moving backward and forward,

    the warm day breaks.

And we think:

at last,

at last,

could it be,

is this true,

did we make this happen?

    Life fills itself to the brim,

    outside and inside our worlds.

TAKING THE WORLD AS IT COMES

Throwing the dice.

Taking the world as it comes.

Walking in the night without a torch.

Approaching the sun at dawn.

Looking outside and inside,

and being overwhelmed

by both these worlds.

IN YOUR WORLD

In your world there are no boundaries.

Everything is possible.

The windows are kept widely open.

Your lovers leave their expectations at your door.

The reality does not crumble.

New thoughts spring to life.

An eye shines from an aperture in the sky.

The landscapes are seen in all their vastness.

There are no violated spaces,

no defining seas,

no laid obstacles on your path.

Every day is different from the other.

Every represented object

is a reduced cosmos.

You manage to interpret every sign.

You remember different episodes,

many spaces of ephemeral moments,

the movement of the seasons.

the soul's monologues,

the lovers' dialogues,

a refuge from reality,

many shadows,

- not all seen and talked of -.

THE POWER OF IMAGINATION

Life goes forward.

It turns its back on the past.

Its pulse beats in the present.

The coasts are numerous.

Your world-view can make them changeable.

Your imagination is a wizard.

It can do anything.

It can preserve a system of illusions

or establish a point of stability.

It can draw a geometric chart,
a circle with the moon, the sun, the planets
and the different stations of life.

It can explain to you why things
turned out the way they did
and predict to you what the future holds in store.

It can concrete your most striking dreams
and make you aware of every particular mood.

It can make you touch the impalpable,
see the invisible and hear the inaudible.

It can give a meaning to every moment.

It can eroticize, sublimate,

turn lovemaking into ceremonies and rites.

>
> The dew of the dawn softens your days.
>
> You know the world.
>
> It knows your heart.

THE DREAM

At the feet of a dream,

truths are blurted out,

the fantasy is picked up,

impressions pour in,

the veil of security is ripped apart.

You do not seek for protection,

you are attuned to the moment.

You cut the navel string

and kick yourself loose from reality.

Your spirit interlinks with space.

The microcosm blends with the macrocosm.

A flash of lightening suddenly blazes at you.

Your vision becomes disoriented,

your freedom claustrophobic.

Different mirrors duplicate your image.

You hear the beating of drums

or a roar of laughter happening at your expense.

Something is wanting.

You break with usual habits.

Your reality is transformed.

Your actions do not follow any formulaic pattern.

Whirling imaginings carry you all through the adventure:

the water shakes itself free,

you are sailing your boat in a lagoon,

you are avoiding the dangerous tide.

You are in search for a place

in which you might find salvation or remedy.

You want to feed on forgetfulness.

Drained specters appear and disappear.

The zones take fire.

You're at risk.

You fly off over airy peaks.

The shadows are reduced,

the tomorrows are conquered.

It is a positive dream.

Your interpretation is not suspect.

You recapitulate the images once again.

The night fades away.

The day breaks.

STAGNATION

There are gestures that do not promise anything,

landscapes that are hard to define,

journeys that do not move forward,

deserted houses,

dispersed birds,

indecipherable signs,

visions without images,

insubstantial thoughts,

unreachable spaces within and outside,

powerless days, weary of books and lights,

people who look alike,

who talk too low or too loud.

WAITING FOR GODOT

"Hell is other people",
Jean-Paul Sartre writes.

There is a hell without any exit
that is reminiscent of a nightmare
in which a prisoner
is unable to imagine a possible future.

Passivity in itself is a hell.
The present is void, motionless,
frozen and gloomy.

An immediate option is to find a savior;

someone who would be comforting and reassuring.

But when the prisoner finds the rescuer,

much to his dismay,

the mirror keeps on sending back

a distorting image.

It's time to find another savior.

The searcher feels lucky today.

He is waiting for Godot,

but Godot doesn't come.

Who is Godot?

Do you know who or what you are waiting for?

A god, a man, a woman, a child,

an animal, a flag, a tree or a stone?

Someone, something, everyone,

everything or nothing?

Everyone is waiting for someone or something.

Everything or everyone is Godot.

Life is meaningless without Godot.

Do you know where Godot is today

and why Godot doesn't come?

I am still waiting for Godot.

You can wait with me if you choose to.

How would life be if Godot came?

I don't know, but it would not be the same.

Many are still waiting for Godot.

There is a beauty in the absurdity of waiting.

There is hope.

Do you know where the exit is?

Do you know where the path is that leads to Godot?

Do you know where the path is that leads to the Self?

CONFLICTS

How strange they are together, he thinks.

Has she thought about that?

She frowns.

She probably has.

They are doing a mess of things again.

Doubt is setting in again.

What's wrong with her
and what's wrong with him?

Does he know her?

Does she know him?

Is she really the one he loves

or has someone else slipped into her place?

"I have changed," she says.

She is right.

Who is she?

Has he ever known her?

They are suddenly in a familiar Bergman's movie,

and the clock is tick tacking,

and they are suffering silently.

Then all of the sudden;

who started it?

He does not remember it well now.

Who brought the thought

which pulled this other thought

that highlighted an obscure one,

blew up a combustible one,

watered a dried out one,

divulged a hidden one,

destroyed a fragile one?

Who knocked down the domino pieces?

Who flung the lion's door open?

Who caused the avalanche?

They both blame

and criticize each other.

They both feel hurt and rejected.

It is almost impossible to make sense of each other.

Why did he choose to stay until the very end?

It was probably out of politeness

or of mere curiosity,

or did he believe in a happy ending?

Outside the sky is a patchwork of pink and purple.

It is too nice an evening to break up.

Would all these arguments bring them back to each other?

Would they understand each other more?

Would the quiet return?

Would she change again?

Would they love each other again?

Would she love him again?

ABSURDISM AND REALISM

Camus and the act devoid of purpose,
the myth of Sisyphus
and the life devoid of meaning.
Kierkegaard and Absurdism.

Frozen aliens.
Lonely paths stretching endlessly.

No interest whatsoever in history,
geography, culture or any movement of the soul.

No love for any woman, man, child or animal.
No feeling of togetherness with anyone or anything.

Weariness about the monotony of the days.

Past, present and future overlap.

Restlessness over the same faces and architectures.

No attractive appeal.

No appealing wilderness.

Deserts outside and inside the homes.

The power to differentiate,

to overcome the invariability,

to find meaning,

to become involved,

to elevate oneself,

to sublimate,

has incomprehensibly been taken away.

SOMEWHERE IN THIS WORLD

I am reading Zola's *Germinal* on the balcony.
I have never seen a mine or miners.
I can however imagine myself being there,
in this monstrous mine
that traps, mutilates and kills its victims.

I am not there however.
The evening falls.
It is half dark around me.

Picasso's *Guernica*.

War is the monster.

Innocents are inflicted,

buildings are wrenched by violence,

soldiers are dismembered,

animals are suffering or dead,

stigmata and skulls are everywhere.

There is always a war raging on somewhere.

I am not there however.

The day breaks.

MEMORIES

A procession of memories
can be interminable.

Like crowds coming out from the dark,
like a sudden flight of birds,
memories can emerge from anywhere;
from anything,
from the door of nothingness,
from extraordinary images and sights,
from simple deeds,
from torments and disorders,
from the clearest thoughts,
from interpretations and associations,
from words and expressions,
from a few written lines,
from in between the lines.

Some of them are refreshing

as a spring,

the colors of a rainbow,

a flowing stream,

a garden with its flowers and trees,

a dear presence,

a soft night,

a promising dawn,

hands joined in prayer,

words and gestures of endearment,

love and all its promises.

Others are as heavy

as the stones of a tower without a door,

a desolate winter,

the cold setting in,

a storm,

a tormenting absence,

a veiled star,

a sigh,

a scream,

a betrayal,

a loss,

a tragedy,

a mourning,

an exile.

SOME GO AND COME

Some go and come as they please.
The world is never too big for them.
Their steps are free.

They are guided mystically to an obscure place,
in which they find the object of their dreams.

They wake up every day in their lover's arms
and use love naturally,
without thinking,
like the air they breathe
and the water they drink.

QUESTIONS ABOUT LOVE

Are there different degrees of love,
different levels,
like there are different shades of shadows,
colors and lights?

Are a few love affairs more suited
for the day and others for the night?

Are there different forms of love?

Glowing and generous,
round like the wheel of the sun;

obsessive and grieving,
flat like a dry desert,
dark like a dark coffin,

blood-sucking like bats
fatal like widow spiders;

rectangular,
in which the lovers
are bound together;

or paradoxically,
two points,
distant and lost in space,
missing a possible encounter
and a shared hope
for a mutual liberation.

Does one choose to love
or does love fall on one
like the apple fell on Newton's head?

Can a love suddenly cease to be?

Is falling out of love a tragedy
and never being able to love again
an even greater tragedy?

SEARCHING FOR A POEM

I have been searching for a poem

in the earth,

in the wind,

in the water,

in the fire,

in the passing clouds,

in the stars spinning,

in the mountain tops,

in the ravines,

in the caverns,

in the shadows,

in the nights,

in the advancing dawns,

in the shifting of the light,

in the vibration of the sound,

behind the doors,

outside of the windows,

in the rooms,

in the departures,

in the arrivals,

in the hotels,

in the houses,

in the world that is pulsating,

in the rivers,

on the roads,

in the cars,

in the trains,

in the planes,

in the ships,

in the sun's rays,

in the rainbows,

in the eclipses,

in the solstices,

in the raindrops,

in the whirlwinds,

in the lightning flashes,

in the volcanic eruptions,
in the falls,
in the roots,
in the flowers,
in the open landscapes,
in the center of the world,
under the stones,
in the quality of your step,
in the dust,
in the hour glass,
in my concrete thoughts,
in your imaginary deeds,
in the turn of your key,
in the sip of wine,
in the melting candle,
in your glare,
in the lines of your hand,
in the smile on your face
in the expressions of love,
in the dialogues,

in the kisses,

in the caresses,

in the silence.

.

SOLACE

In order to keep you warm
I have painted a fire on the wall.

Can you see it?
Can you feel its strength?

I put in it everything the summer gave me:
its heat, its landscapes,
its noises, its flavors and its perfumes.

Around you,
nature is an artist.

The soft sun
weighs so light on the fields.

If you touch the earth,

the mud and gold blend together.

You cannot say that the sky is void.

THE MAGICAL DAYS

The snow glistens under the sunlight.

All along the roads of happiness,
the days open their arms for us.

The colors shift.
New births defy the void.

Our dreams become clearer,

We are transformed
by the unity of our intensity.

The towns, which welcome us now,

remember other towns.

A new union is formed.

We are as much affected by the world

as it is by us.

Our thoughts and feelings

spread out in all directions.

The lights flirt in the nights.

We kiss the same horizons.

Our faith and hope make us smile.

PAST AND CURRENT POTENTIAL LIVES

I wonder sometimes about past lives,

- if such lives existed

and if I had the opportunity of living them –.

I imagine myself pushing on a secret button

and seeing them all flashing on a screen.

Curiously, like a spectator,

I will see myself in other times,

in other surroundings,

with other persons,

- parents, possible spouses,

children, colleagues, rivals -.

I will see my different faces,

listen to my different voices,

study my different thoughts and deeds.

I will see myself as a farmer in one life,

a fisherman in the life before that,

married in one life, single in another,

old in one life, young in another.

I will be acquainted with these other me, -

these other selves that will coincide with my current self. -

I will feel bound to them all

and will long to reach their utmost depths.

After my past lives,

I will wonder about my potential current ones.

I will go through many different choices and deeds

and see these lives flashing on the screen.

This is what would have happened

if I had made this special choice

and acted in this specific manner

on this specific occasion;

if I had opened one door instead of closing it

or closed another one instead of opening it;

if I had expressed my feelings when I didn't

or didn't express them when I did;

if I had been courageous when I was a coward

and a coward when I was courageous;

this is how my life would be

if I had stayed at home on this special afternoon

instead of going out and meeting this special friend

who became responsible of the direction my life took;

and this is how my life would be today

if I had gone out on another day

instead of staying at home

and meeting this other person,

unknown to me today.

Rome, Paris, Texas, a desert,

a hotel, a house, a flat, a tent,

famous, poor, wealthy,

married, single, divorced,

alive, gone.

Some deeds would have given me better lives

others not,

some would have been fatal.

- I would never know -.

INANIMATE THINGS

Perhaps that the red flower
likes to absorb the writer's poetic mood,
that the yellow one is bored to death
and enjoys only music,

that the chair longs to be sat on
and the phone likes to ring,

that the books want to be opened,
the pages insist on being turned,
and the intentions long to be revealed,

Perhaps that the wall papers and the carpets
talk a silent language
that wants to be interpreted,

that the objects around us
have their ways of communication,
their moods and impressions,
their likes and dislikes,
their drives and energies.

DRIVE

A desire that takes shape.

A circle of light

divided into two half-moons

which play together,

combine and become a heart.

A staring face

eclipsed by a sudden shadow,

which becomes veiled

and then illuminated.

A body filled with rays,

a noise embodied,

a thirst materialized,

a soul surfacing,

an inner movement,

the restlessness of the gests,

the spinning of a circle around a void,

an incalculable formula,

the erasure of a division,

the expansion of the thoughts,

the impulsiveness of the drive,

a boomerang thrown in the air and returning.

Millions of seconds passing without a break,

dissymmetric, unpredictable,

deviating in their course,

exceeding the limits,

always free and untamed

in a rotating world.

REFLECTIONS

No transparent shadows exist
unless they are ghosts.

The ones who are accustomed to wear masks
are looking for different masks.

When they open their mouths to talk
their vagueness is extremely fascinating.

Does time really exist
or do all times exist simultaneously?

Each world contains its different shapes,
heights, depths, orders, powers, balances,
chaos, flashing insights, inner defenses,
vulnerabilities and breakdowns.

Awareness should not be forgotten:
neither the cosmic awareness
nor the unifying one.

The awareness of living
and the time passing
are like pulsing veins
running through everything,

The sense of gravity
makes us aware of the presence of the elements.

The universe adapts itself to gravity

as much as gravity adapts itself to the universe.

Light discharges the sun

and charges the earth.

The best memories are the shortest ones.

Nothing should be taken lightly.

Everything is related to something else.

Somewhere close

and somewhere beyond,

language turns in its own world.

Two persons who live far away from each other,

can discover the same truths.

Each one of them is a satellite
for the other one's frequencies.

Electric waves pass between them
through an invisible opening.

Their ideas can fuse together on the spot.

POSSIBILITIES

If the path is endless

it is so that we can find each other on it.

Every shared thought

tingles with possibilities.

There is no movement

if there is no duration

A movement can stretch out

and withdraw

in every imaginable direction.

Order and chaos

take up space.

The horizontal and vertical
can expand and dissolve.

Roads can ascend and decline,
Horizons can advance and step back,
Hills can rise and withdraw.

The existence of an island
reduces the size of the sea.

Reality can be turned
into an imaginary desert
and vice versa.

A returning wave
is filled with energy .

Life has always something to give
for those who do not leave the scene.

The beauty of being
is gratified to everyone and everything.

www.ingramcontent.com/pod-product-compliance
Lightning Source LLC
Chambersburg PA
CBHW022305060426
42446CB00007BA/597